Books purchased with funds from
The Blessing Foundation
for project coordinated by BRCN Student,
Morgan A. Schone

Born With A Broken Heart®

By Rick and Annette Gallegos

Illustrated by John Shallenberger

www.alexheartfund.com

AuthorHouse™
1663 Liberty Drive
Bloomington, IN 47403
www.authorhouse.com
Phone: 1-800-839-8640

© 2010 Rick and Annette Gallegos. All rights reserved.

No part of this book may be reproduced, stored in a retrieval system, or transmitted by any means without the written permission of the author.

First published by AuthorHouse   12/29/2010

ISBN: 978-1-4490-3760-4 (sc)

Library of Congress Control Number: 2010900774

Printed in the United States of America
Bloomington, Indiana

This book is printed on acid-free paper.

In memory of Alexander Xavier Gallegos

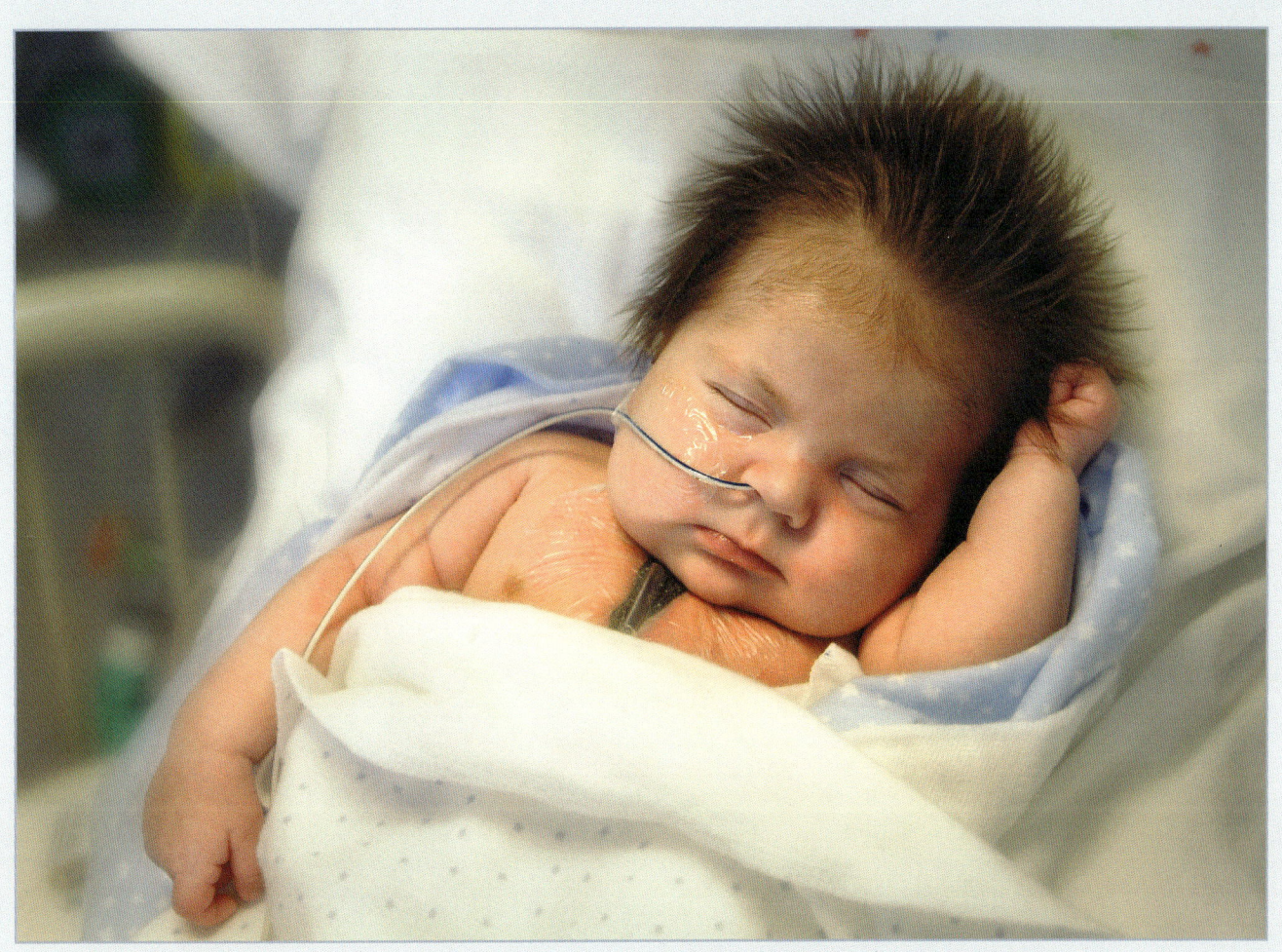

About the Book

Alex's heart book, _Born With A Broken Heart_, is an inspirational and educational children's book. It is our hope that this book will give parents and children the opportunity to learn about Congenital Heart Disease (CHD) and to spread CHD awareness throughout the world. It is also our wish that the courage and spirit Alex showed in life will inspire others who face challenges to do so with faith, passion, and unconditional love.

This book will be available through the following websites:

1) http://www.authorhouse.com

2) http://www.alexheartfund.com

3) Facebook Causes - Children's Heart Fund in Memory of Alexander Xavier Gallegos

Illustrated by: John Shallenberger

100% Profit will go to the Children's Heart Fund in Memory of Alexander Xavier Gallegos at Cedars-Sinai Medical Center.

Acknowledgments

Greg Fontana, M.D., Alex's brilliant heart surgeon at Cedars-Sinai Medical Center and Jan, our contact in Community Relations: Thank you for the children's book idea.

Kristina Garcia-Stack, a close friend and teacher at NACC Charter School. Thank you for your time and effort and a special thanks to your students for their comments and suggestions. We are grateful for their patience and valuable insight.

Thank you to our illustrator, John Shallenberger. Without your wonderful illustrations, this book would not be complete. Your creativity and talent are superb! We are forever grateful for your dedication, compassion, and generosity.

To children with Congenital Heart Disease (CHD):

It is not your fault you were born with a heart condition. Thankfully, there are special doctors and nurses that have the training to help you get better. There are a lot of children that are born with heart conditions who have to have surgery to fix the problem. Some of you get to go home while others, like Alex, go to heaven.

Alyssa, our little healer: We don't know what we would be doing today if not for you.

And finally, to our family and friends for your love, support, and encouragement in the creation of Alex's heart book, we thank you!

This book was inspired by Alex's beautiful smile and his strong will to live. He experienced many close calls while in the hospital and survived those critical times because of the love and care he received from family, friends, and the staff of Cedars-Sinai Medical Center.

Alex, our little angel, we wish you were still with us so that you could continue to enrich our lives with your giggles and laughter. Your love and smiles were contagious. This book has been created in your memory.

Mom and Dad say babies come from heaven.

My brother, Alex, was in mommy's tummy and almost ready to come into this world. Her belly grew with my brother inside it, and I could hardly wait until he was born.

Dad took Mom to the hospital so my brother could be born and so he could drive her home afterward.

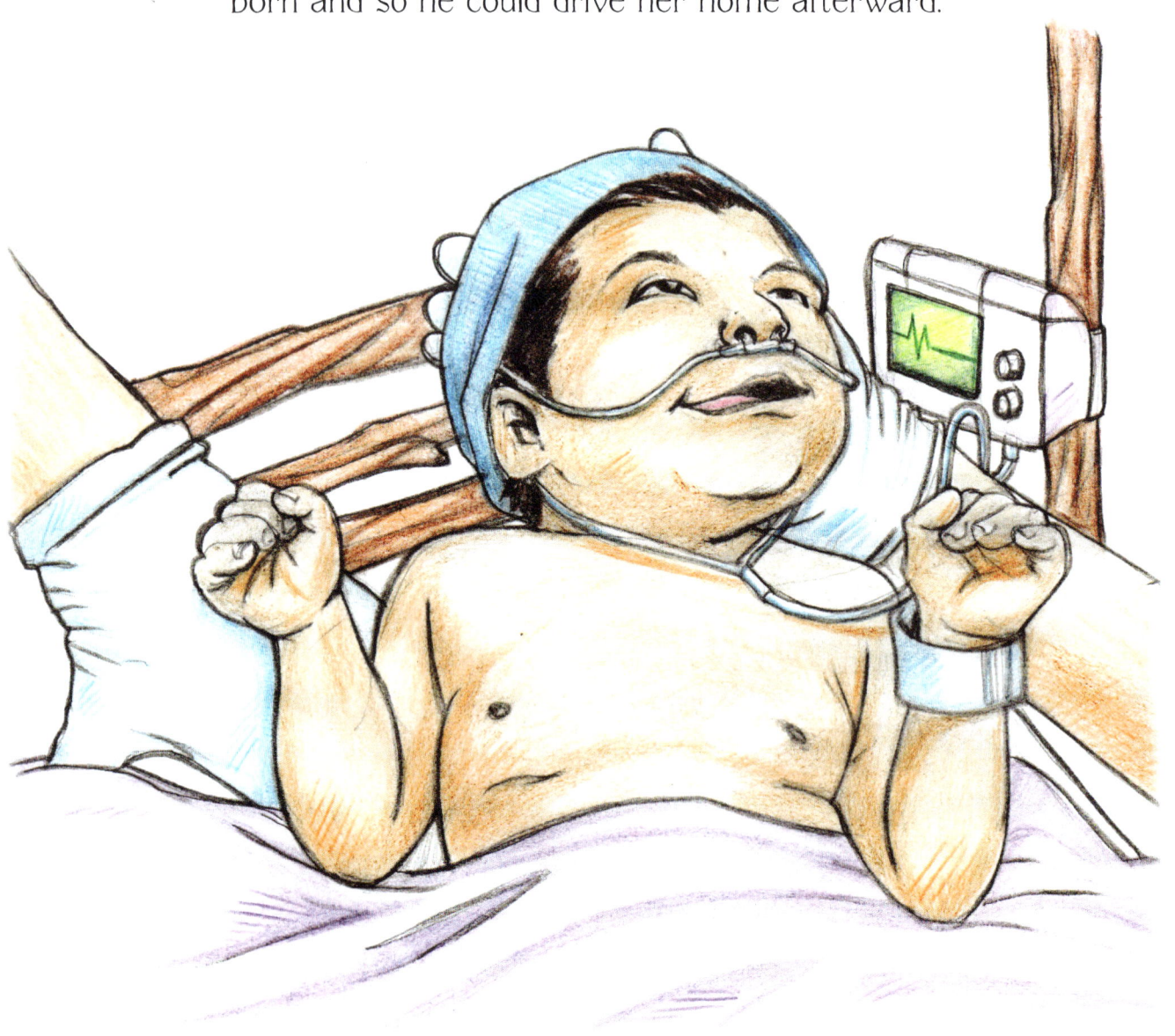

After we had waited a long time, a heart surgeon said that my brother would not be able to go home that day because he had an owie in his heart.

The doctor said that Alex had a hole in his heart that needed to be repaired.

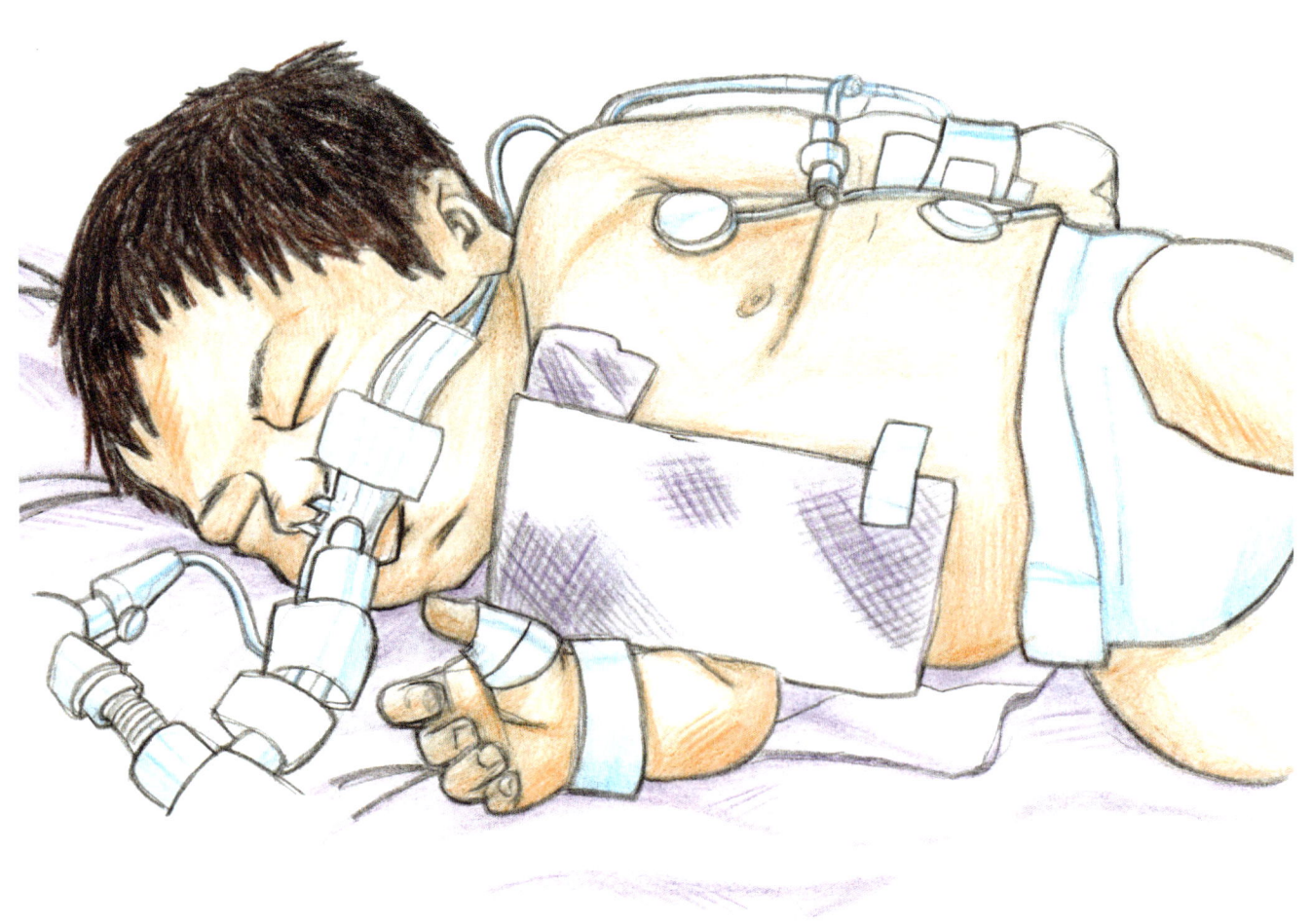

The owie in his heart made oxygen-poor blood mix in the heart, making it hard for him to breathe.

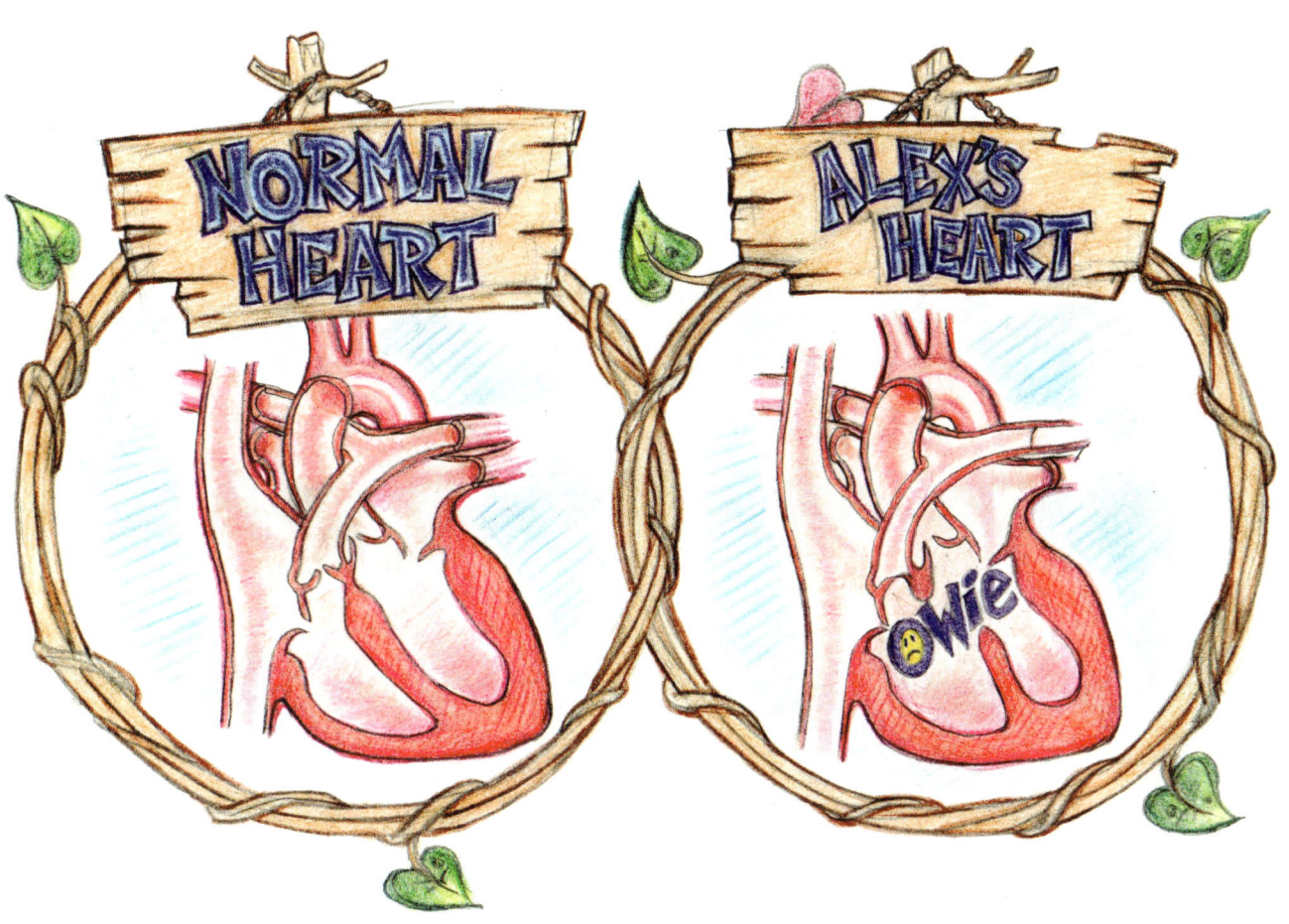

Mom and Dad were worried about my brother because he would have to stay a while longer in the hospital so the doctors could fix the owie in his heart.

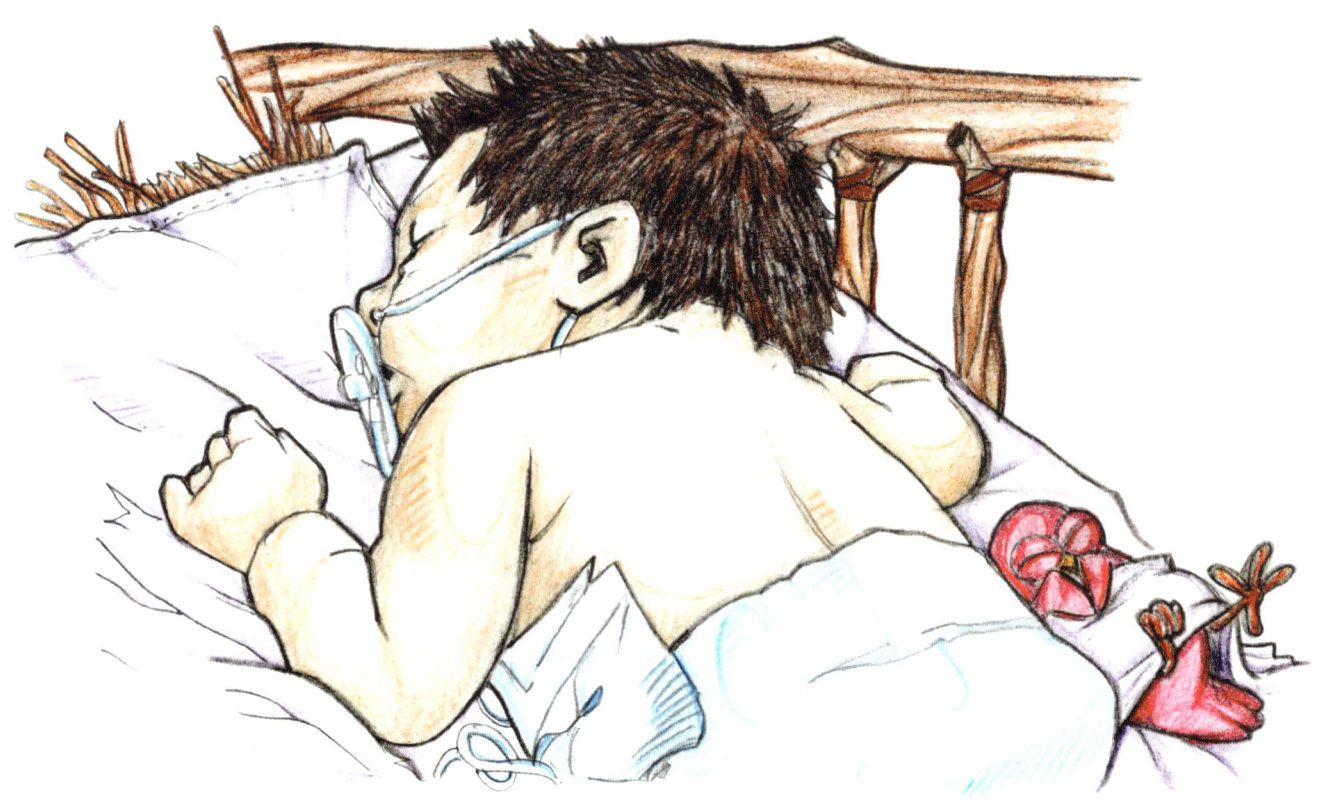

We had to go home without him. They said it would take a long operation to fix the owie in my brother's heart.

The doctor took my brother to a special operating room to repair his heart.

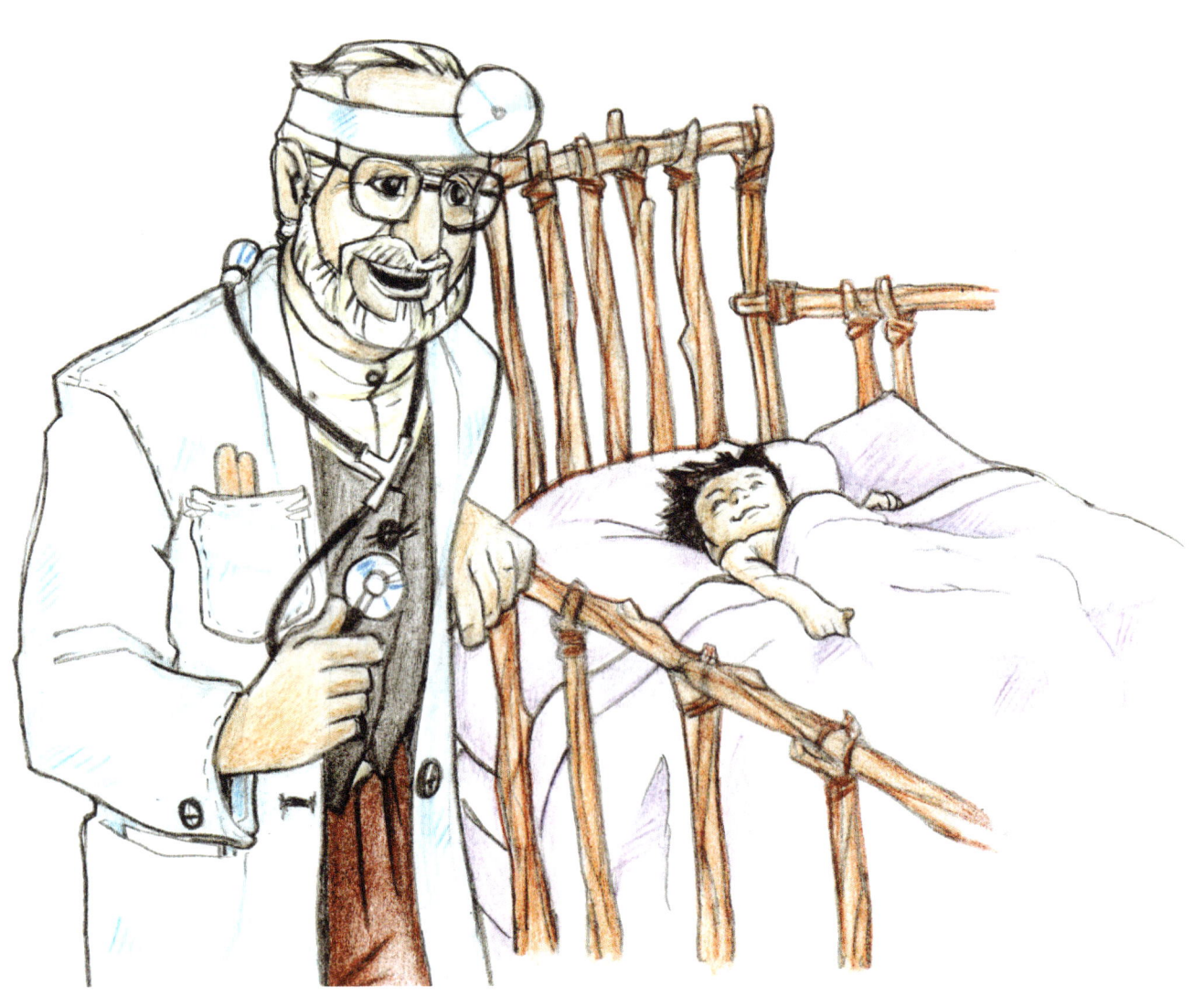

Mom and Dad said a prayer for my brother.

We had to wait a long time in the waiting room. We were worried because Alex had been in the operating room for a long time. Mom and Dad felt assured that he would be fine.

After we had waited for a long time, the doctor came out to let us know that my brother had done well and was recovering.

Seeing Alex with all the tubes and machines attached to him made Mom and Dad sad. They were told the machines were there to help him get better.

Leaving Alex at the hospital was hard for Mom and Dad, but until he was well enough to come home after many weeks, they would have to visit him there.

Alex eventually began to feel much better, so he was finally allowed to come home!

Being home for the first time excited my brother!

For many months, a physical therapist worked with my brother so he could roll, sit, crawl, stand, and walk like you and I.

At age one, Alex had his second major heart surgery.

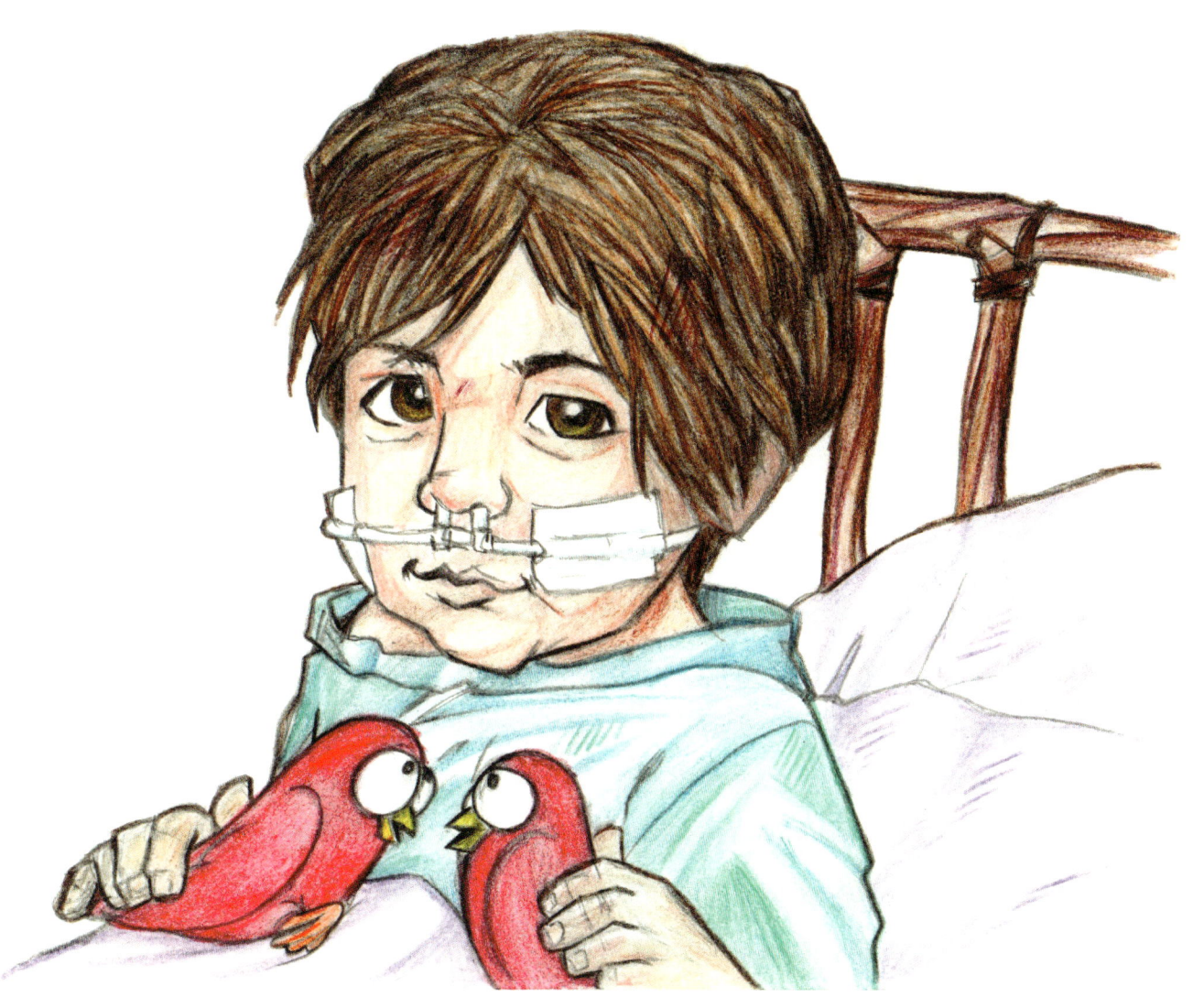

Even after his second major heart surgery, my brother was able to play and have lots of fun!

Fun was his game; he loved to make others smile.

Right before his second birthday, Alex learned to walk by himself.

My brother loved walking so much because it made him happy.

We visited family for my brother's second birthday; he was so happy.

Several days later, Alex became very sick and God took him to heaven.

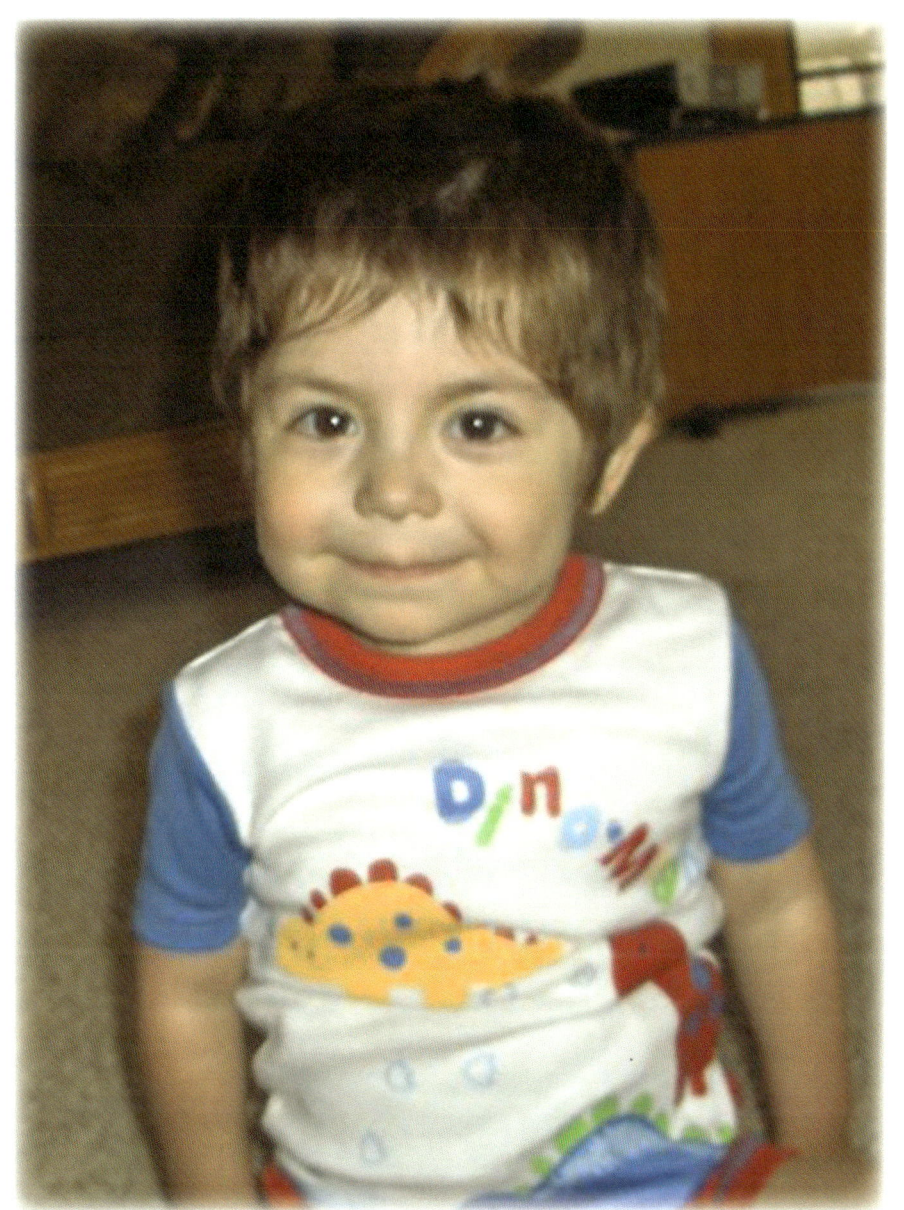

Mom and Dad say it is good to think about my brother in heaven because someday we will be with him again.

Until then, we will keep him in our hearts and remember his giggles and laughter.

Mom and dad say my brother no longer has to see the doctor, because he is having fun playing and walking in heaven.

He is keeping the angels busy chasing after him. So don't be sad for my brother, Alex. He would not want anyone to feel that way because he is happy in heaven.

Many children with heart conditions have surgery to fix their hearts. Most get to go home and live long, happy lives. Others, like Alex, go to heaven.

The Children's Heart Fund in Memory of Alexander Xavier Gallegos has been established at Cedars-Sinai Medical Center!

This fund will provide financial assistance to families of "blue babies" who, like Alex, are born with a heart condition that makes them turn bluish or purplish from a lack of oxygen. Some of these families travel many miles so that their babies can receive the specialized care that they need at Cedars-Sinai Medical Center.

The Children's Heart Fund will be managed by Alex's heart surgeon, Dr. Greg Fontana. It will help families in need with costs for medications, gas, meals, and lodging while their babies are in the hospital.

Our hope is that the Children's Heart Fund will continue to grow every year so that it can ultimately be large enough to fund important medical research in pediatric cardiology as well. We would also like this fund to cover the transportation and escorting costs for one child each year to travel to Cedars-Sinai Medical Center from Central or South America to receive heart surgery that is unavailable to them in their country.

For now, however, we are grateful to help families in smaller, but still significant, ways.

CHD Survivor's

Aidan Kristopher Laforest
Hypoplastic Left Heart Syndrome (HLHS)

and

Scarlett Antoinette Pomaville
Tetralogy of Fallot with Pulmonary Atresia
(also called Pulmonary Atresia VSD with MAPCAs).

A Special Survivor Dedication to the LaForest family for sharing Aidan's story with us.

Aidan Kristopher LaForest was born with half of a heart; this is called Hypoplastic Left Heart Syndrome (HLHS).

After a normal and healthy pregnancy, our son Aidan was born with an undetected heart defect. Aidan was born with hypoplastic left heart syndrome, or half a heart. We have seen him through three open heart surgeries, three heart catheterizations (one being very invasive), many other minor procedures, many unexpected ER visits, and a dental procedure in the OR. Aidan is a thriving, fun, and very energetic five-year-old who loves life and everyone around him. He has big brown eyes and a smile that lights every room he enters. We call his scar the door to his heart, and we tell everyone who will listen about his special heart.

Aidan has a little brother, Gabriel, who has a healthy heart. They play and fight well together, and they are the best of friends! Aidan and Gabriel welcomed their baby sister, Isabelle, in March of 2010. Thankfully, she too has a healthy heart. The boys love her so much and are so very proud. Aidan has many restrictions: no day care or preschool (because of the risk of infection), no contact sports or hard blows to his chest. He takes several daily medications and breathing treatments. He will always have to take an antibiotic before any dental procedure or surgery, and he will need to follow his doctors and specialists very closely. Our families have learned so much through Aidan's heart: to love more, to give more, to have patience, not to take things for granted, and to be more faithful. Simply put, we have all become better people! Raising awareness about heart defects (the number-one type of birth defect) is extremely important to our families.

Kristopher & Jamie, proud parents of Aidan
Gabriel, little brother to Aidan &
Isabelle, little sister to Aidan

Hope for Hearts
http://www.causes.com/causes/320927?recruiter_id=69983054

A Special Survivor Dedication to the Pomaville Family for sharing Scarlett's story with us.

Looking at Scarlett Antoinette Pomaville one would never suspect that she has a complex congenital heart defect known as Tetralogy of Fallot with Pulmonary Atresia (also called Pulmonary Atresia VSD with MAPCAs).

Our heart story began when I was referred to have a fetal echocardiogram because a routine ultrasound revealed I had a Single Umbilical Artery. At 25 weeks gestation, I was told that Scarlett would require open-heart surgery within days of being born in order to survive, and that she would have heart issues her entire life which would require life-long care with a cardiologist.

Barely a newborn, Scarlett had her first open-heart surgery at 8 days old. In order for her heart to pump blood to the lungs to pick up oxygen, she needed a donor pulmonary valve implanted in her heart. Unfortunately, since it is from a cadaver, it will not grow with her; therefore, she had her second open-heart surgery at 7 months. My husband and I had to quickly adapt to being caregivers for a special needs child. We learned how to insert a feeding tube, how to use a pulse-ox machine, and oxygen tank, and how to fortify her milk. For the first 7 months of her life, she saw a cardiologist every 2 weeks. I never thought we had it in us, but Scarlett has given us the strength to overcome any challenges thrown our way. She is truly our inspiration.

Because of Scarlett's heart condition, I became a huge advocate for CHDs. My license plate says "HRTMOM", because I am proud to be a heartmom to Scarlett. I spread awareness wherever I can and provide support to parents whose child has been diagnosed with a CHD. As for Scarlett, she will have to undergo at least 2 more surgeries before she's a teenager to replace the donor valve that will not grow with her.

Today (after 2 surgeries), Scarlett is pinker than ever and doing fantastic. She is off of the feeding tube and the oxygen. Her favorite thing to do is play with her older sister Violet, and the family cat, Cupcake. She runs, climbs, dances, claps, babbles and is an overall happy and thriving toddler. She is small for her age, but doing great.

Thank you for reading our story.

Melodie, Todd, Violet and Scarlett Pomaville

A Special Angel Dedication to the Dereksen's family
for sharing their sweet Tommy's story with us.

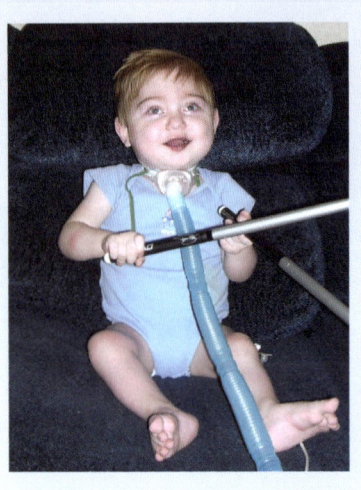

My son Thomas "Tommy" Lee Dereksen came crashing into the world 7 weeks premature with a fighter spirit and a wonderful cry. Diagnosed during my pregnancy, we were prepared he would have heart defects. His first echo confirmed this and gave us our complete diagnosis. Double Inlet Left Ventricle, Transposition of the Great Arteries, Severe Pulmonary Stenosis, Ventricle Septal Defect and Patent Ductus Arteriosus. He would spend the first 79 days of his life in the hospital not dealing with being a preemie, but having heart surgery, being diagnosed with a birth defect to his esophagus, getting a G-tube and getting a tracheostomy (trach). Recovery after heart surgery was terrible filled with infections and lung issues. We were so happy to finally have our little guy home!

For the next 6 months, we learned to adjust to a medically fragile child. Occupational and physical therapies were started. Tommy dealt with sensory issues and loathed touch. His care was 24/7. He was hooked to monitors at home, was fed with a pump, and was given medications about every 4 hours around the clock. Despite it all, Tommy grew and learned to love us as much as we did him. He smiled for the first time at 5 months old, and allowed me to rock him to sleep for the first time at 7 months old. We even took a trip out of state to visit our families. Finally the time came for the second stage of his heart surgery.

The day came for Tommy's heart cath. Everyone was excited to see the day Tommy would have his Glenn and be on his way to a repaired heart. However, his heart cath gave us very bad news. Tommy had secondary pulmonary hypertension, scarring in his lungs, reactive airway disease, and asthma! The Glenn was out of the question. Instead, Tommy's surgeon revised his shunt to give Tommy's body time to grow and hopefully outgrow his lung issues. There was a downside. Tommy would now be oxygen dependant. He came home tethered to about 15 feet of blue tubing and an oxygen concentrator, but he was alive and doing well!

The next year was spent growing, laughing and learning. He had his therapies every week and eventually learned to sit on his own and how to stack and throw things. He had surgery on his esophagus to learn to swallow and began speech therapy. He also had surgery on his trachea so that his airway could be open enough to learn to speak and eventually get out his trach. Tommy learned to sign several words and to verbalize just one, "Mama". He became a huge fan of his exersaucer, signing "jump" several times a day until we gave in. He would clap with delight and blow us kisses whenever we obliged him.

In July, 2008, Tommy went into the hospital. He was treated for a bout of pseudomonas, which is a bacteria that lives in the trachea and can flare up with illness. After his recovery, his doctors proceeded with a tonsillectomy and adenoid removal to give him an even larger airway. Tommy did wonderfully! A few days later, he was off oxygen for the first time in a year and breathing on his own with his trach capped off. We began discussing the Glenn again, but the trach had to come out first. His doctors didn't want to risk infection with an incision that close to the trach site. The trach came out on a Monday and on Wednesday we were home!

Being home was short-lived. That Friday, Tommy was admitted again for respiratory distress. His trach was put back in. He was again requiring oxygen and no one was able to tell me why. He was very sick and I was not getting the answers I was looking for. I got the answers in a way no parent should ever get them. By autopsy. Tommy died Wednesday, August 20, 2008. One minute he was sitting in his crib, playing and watching his favorite movie on TV. He had a breathing treatment and again went into respiratory distress. He did not recover and a crash cart was called. The team worked on him for 45 minutes, but he was already gone. The autopsy showed Tommy had been in heart failure and an undiagnosed case of bronchopneumonia caused his already sick heart to go into a lethal arrhythmia. He was 5 days away from being 23 months old.

Chanin Rene Dereksen - Tommy's Mother

Tommy Dereksen Memorial Fund
http://www.causes.com/causes/312677?recruiter_id=16595106

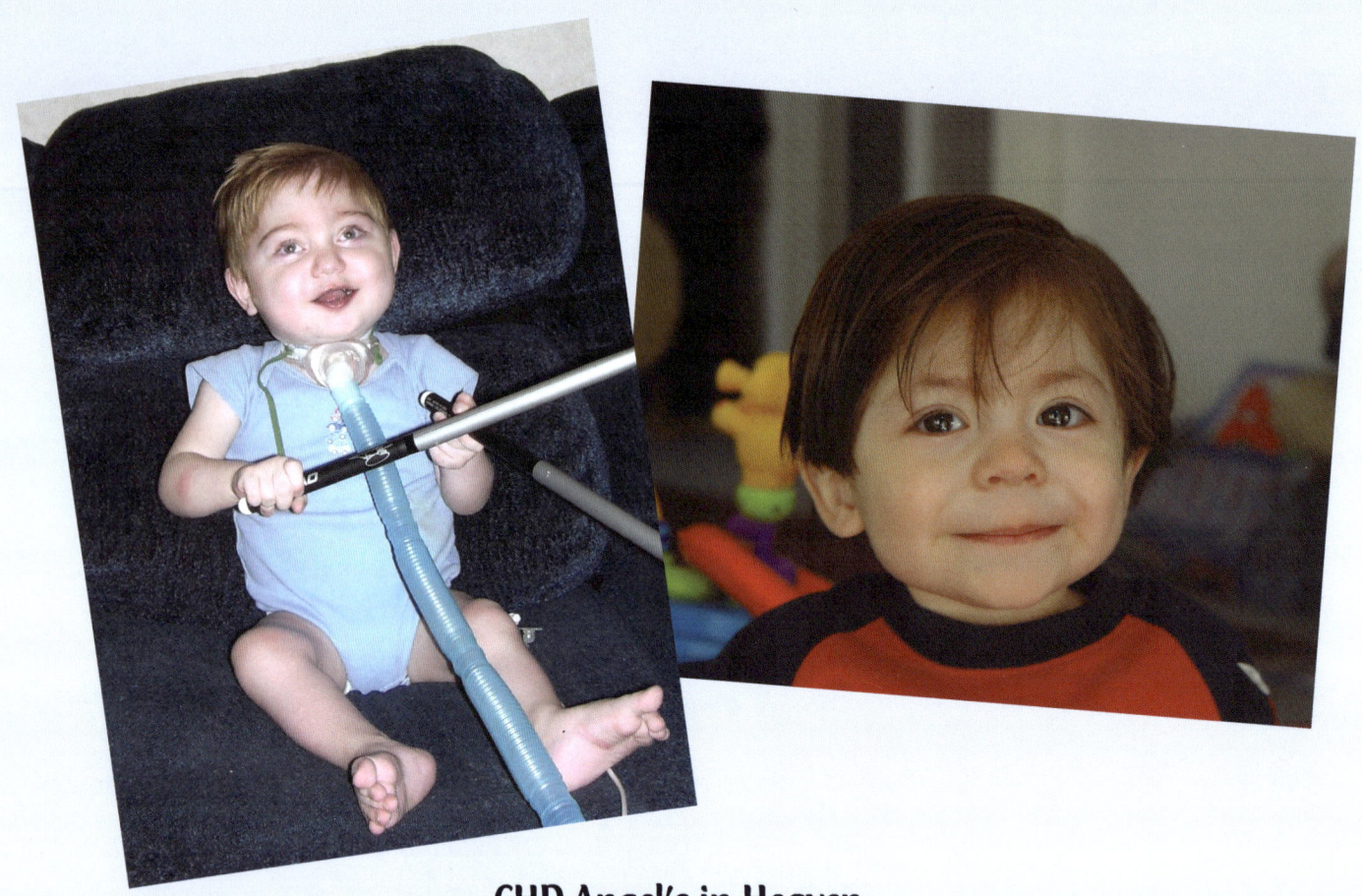

CHD Angel's in Heaven

Thomas "Tommy" Lee Dereksen
TGA, DILV, VSD, ASD, PDA
Sever Pulmonary Stenosis, Cricopharygeal Achalasia,
Trach, G-tube, Asthma, Pulmonary Hypertension
Chronic Lung Disease, Reactive Airway Disease

and

Alexander Xavier Gallegos
Tetralogy of Fallot with Pulmonary Atresia

CHD Survivor's and Angel's

Angel – Thomas "Tommy" Lee Dereksen

Survivor – Aidan Kristopher Laforest

Survivor – Scarlett Antoinette Pomaville

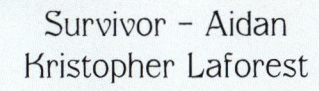

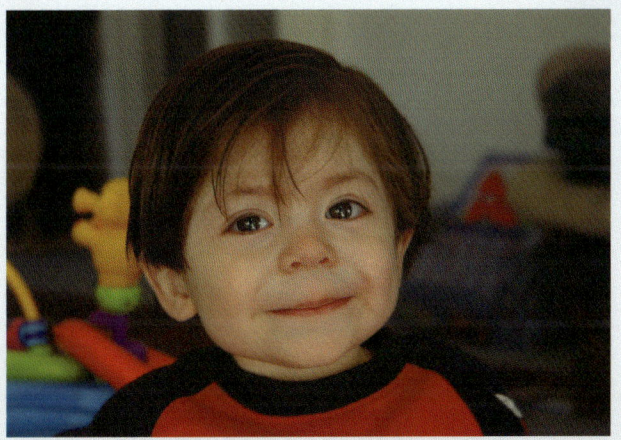

Angel – Alexander Xavier Gallegos

Survivors & Angels

A Special Honor to Alex's heart friends: CHD Survivor's & Angel's

Common Heart Condition Legend

- Congenital Heart Disease (**CHD**)
- Hypoplastic Left Heart Syndrome (**HLHS**)
- Tetralogy of Fallot (**TOF**)
- Pulmonary Stenosis (**PS**)
- Hypoplastic Right Heart Syndrome (**HRHS**)
- Tricuspid Atresia (**TA**)
- Atrial Septal Defect (**ASD**)
- Ventricular Septal Defect (**VSD**)
- Coarctation of the Aorta (**COA**)
- Bicuspid Aortic Valve (**BAV**)
- Double Outlet Right Ventricle (**DORV**)
- Atrial Septal Defect (**ASD**)
- Mitral Valve Replacement (**MVR**)
- Pulmonary Atresia (**PA**)
- Pulmonary Stenosis (**PS**)
- Major Aorta Pulmonary Collateral Arteries (**MAPCA**)
- Atrioventricular Canal Defect (**AVCD**)
- Transposition of Great Arteries (**TGA**)
- Double Chamber Right Ventricle (**DCRV**)
- Double Inlet Left Ventricle (**DILV**)
- Patent Ductus Arteriosus (**PDA**)
- Atrioventricular Septal Defect (**AVSD**)

A

Aaron Tanner
HLHS with Left Atrial Isomerism and Single Ventricle
April 8, 2005

Abby Wardell
TOF with severe PS
January 18, 2000

Adam Sallee
HLHS with Coronary Artery Fistula
June 6, 2010

Addison Kristine Bennett
TOF
December 16, 2008

Aiden Michael Daugherty
HRHS/TA/ASD/VSD/PS
July 10, 2009

Aidan Ronald Pearsall
HLHS
May 22, 2008

Alexander Dante
COA/BAV
July 25, 2005

Alexander Guy Jaworski
HLHS
August 11, 1994

Alexia Boesen
DORV/VSD/PS
December 29, 1985

Alyssa Roze
TOF
November 13, 2009

Anakin Williams
ASD/MVR/LVP
May 27, 2006

Angel Tadeo Parra
TOF/PA/ MAPCA/VSD/DiGeorge Syndrome
November 6, 2006

Aoife Sadhbh Nolan
Shone's Complex
October 22, 2008

A Special Honor to Alex's heart friends: CHD Survivor's & Angel's

Aryn James Mann
HLHS
January 28, 2008 - April 29, 2008

Auriana Faith Reyes
Complete AVCD/Down Syndrome
September 17, 2008

Ava Elaine Allen
TA/TGA/2 VSD's/ASD
December 13, 2008

B

Bela Grace Milne
HLHS
February 29, 2008

Bianca Alexis Salazar
DCRV/VSD
February 18, 2001

Bianca Lopez
TA
May 20, 2007

Brayden Easley
TOF
September 29, 2008

C

Cameron Edward Ulrich
DORV/VSD/AV Discordance/Heart Block/Situs Inversus
June 15, 2006

Carla Morgan Wright
HLHS
April 2, 2007

Carl Edward "Eddie" Kennedy IV
DORV/PA
March 9, 2008

Carl Vito LaSala
HLHS
July 11, 1999 - July 19, 1999

Caylee Rodenbaugh
HLHS
June 26, 2009

Caylen Joan Ayscue
HLHS with Heterotaxy, Dextrocardia, TGA/VSD/Atrial Ventricular Discordance/DORV/PS/Sick Sinus Node Syndrome/Sick AV Node Syndrome/ Malrotated Intestines
June 27, 2007

Charlie R. Grauber Jr.
HRHS/DILV/Stroke Survivor
March 2, 2008

Christopher Lawrence Pena, Jr.
Dilated Left Ventricular non compacted cardiomyopathy/ cyclic neutropenia secondary to Barth Syndrome
April 25, 2008
http://www.caringbridge.org/visit/cj08

Christy
TOF
August 1977

Collin
TGA/Single Ventricle-HLHS
July 24, 2008

Conner Jackson/Williams
LVP/MVR/ASD/Multiple CHD's/heart failure
October 13, 2001 - October 13, 2001

A Special Honor to Alex's heart friends: CHD Survivor's & Angel's

Connor Winchester
HLHS/Epilepsy/PLE
May 1, 2003 - December 13, 2009

Cora Mae McCormick
Complex CHD's
November 30, 2009 - December 6, 2009

C.R Samuel Fields
Shone's Syndrome
December 1, 1998 - May 4, 1999

D

Danny Rivera
HLHS
October 8, 2009

Dean McIlwraith
Collapsed with Critical Aortic Valve Stenosis
June 30, 2009

Delvin James Reeder
TOF/PA
October 17, 2007

Donald Jensen, Jr.
HLHS
December 18, 1993

Dounya Mouhsine
Complete AVSD
August 16, 2008

E

Ella Phillips
PA with IVS
August 7, 2009

Erin Lowrance
ASD/PS/Thymectomy possibly linked to OHS
Adult CHD'er

Ethan Jewel Tanner
Hypotropic Cardiomyopathy
January 29, 2003 - May 20, 2005

F

Fearn Helen Kennan
HLHS
October 28, 2008

Fiona Grace Saurez
COA with arch hypoplasia/PDA/PFO/BAV/AS/Cardiomyopathy
April 28, 2009

G

Gabby Darkhand
TOF
November 1, 2005

Gabrielle Charlize
HLHS/DORV w/transposition/complete heart block/ASD/Mital/Pulmonary Stenosis/Heterotaxy
February 12, 2008

Gwen Wright
TOF/PS/ICD placement/Stoke Survivor
Adult CHD'er

H

Hailey Madisen Howard
TOF/ASD/PFO/DiGeorge Syndrome/Juvenile Rhuematoid Arthritis/Stroke Survivor
December 24, 2005

A Special Honor to Alex's heart friends: CHD Survivor's & Angel's

Haley Alyssa Bishop
Truncus Arteriosus
July 28, 1988

Hazel Hunt
TGA

Holly Jones
PA/VSD/Complex MAPCA's
October 12, 2008

Hope Rebekah McLernon
HRHS/TA/PS
April 25, 2007
"Where there is faith, There is HOPE, and where there is HOPE miracles occur." - unknown

Hope Ruth Matthews
HLHS
April 27, 2010 - April 28, 2010

I

Iolan William Richards
TGA/VSD/PS/sub PS/BPV
December 11, 2007

Isaac Dauphin
COA/Parachute Mitral Valve/Subaortic Stenosis/with Bicuspid Mitral Valve/ Hypoplasia of the Transverse Arch

Isabella Rose Hayes
HLHS
September 17, 2009 - July 21, 2010

Izabella Rose Brancato
TOF
May 19, 2006

J

Jack Christopher Scarfo
TOF
April 15, 2008

Jack Malcolm Linfield
Total Anomalous Pulmonary Venous Connection (Supracardiac)/ASD
November 5, 2005

Jacob Jude Frankum
TA/TGA/Hypoplastic Aorta
April 9, 2010

Jacob Skurjunis
TOF/VSD/PS
August 19, 2006

Jae-Jae Kaehne
HLHS
August 22, 2007

Jake Alan Dennison
HLHS
January 21, 2009 - February 9, 2009
www.tylerelizabethdennison.blogspot.com

James Everett Horner
PA/DILV/Levo-Transposition of the Great Arteries (L-TGA)
September 13, 2007

Jamiee Lynn
Shone's complex
August 7, 2007

Jarod Scott Davis
HLHS
June 2, 1998

A Special Honor to Alex's heart friends: CHD Survivor's & Angel's

Jarret Timothy Coronado Quentin
Shone's Complex/*Jacobsen Syndrome*
January 2, 2005

Jayden John Patrick Corley
TOF
December 8, 2004

Jessica Goffard
TA/VSD/ASD MVP
October 3, 1989

John, 22
*TOF/Pulmonary Valve Replacement/
atenolol for arrhythmias*

Jonah David Cox
DORV/TGA/VSD/COA
July 19, 2009 - August 6, 2009

Jonah Quinton Fite
*TA/VSD/PFO/TGA/Subaortic Stenosis/
COA/Leaky Mitral Valve*
August 12, 2009

Joseph Edwin Lopez Tavares
HLHS with Intact Atrial Septum
December 23, 2005

Joseph Scalise
TOF
July 7, 2003

Josephine Simone
HLHS
September 16, 2005

Joshua Koziol
TOF/VSD/PS/small ASD
March 2009

K

Kaiden Nehemiah Ramsey
HLHS/Heart Transplant Recipient
September 26, 2009

Kamdon Boe
HLHS
March 31, 2007

Karly Boyda
Aortic Stenosis/BAV/COA/Subaortic Stenosis
July 29, 2004

Kassaundra Lynn LaMay
TGA/VSD/ASD/PDA/Arterial Switch
April 25, 2008

Kenzie Hummel
HLHS
November 12, 2009

Kian Barker-Barrs
*HLHS/Bilateral SVC/Central Pulmonary Arterial
Stenosis - Proximal to Hilar Bifurcation/RPA/LPA*
February 5, 2008

Klayton Leary
HLHS/ASD
November 29, 2001

Kristen Seal
ASD/VSD
November 2, 2009

Kylah Sard
MVP
April 29, 1997

A Special Honor to Alex's heart friends: CHD Survivor's & Angel's

Kyle David Caperton
PA/VSD/TOF/DiGeorge Syndrome
January 4, 2007

Kyle Gerald Smith
HLHS/TGA/PS/Dextrocardio
September 8, 2004 - September 22, 2004
Kyle underwent surgery to place a shunt. He fought very hard after his surgery, but sadly earned his angel wings 14 days later on September 22, 2004. We miss him so very much!

L

Laney Grace Chance
TOF/MAPCA
May 6, 2008

Lauren Celeskey
HRHS/TA
August 25, 1987
Adult CHD'er

Liam Dorans
Truncus Arteriosus/type 2/VSD's with Pulmonary Steniosus
November 21, 2004

Liam Tberiouse Scott
HLHS/PA/VSD
July 13, 2010 - July 30, 2010

Lilliann Rose Ferretti
HLHS
October 30, 2008

Lilly Grace Smitsky
TOF/PA with large VSD
June 30, 2009

London Mobley II
HLHS
July 28, 2000

Luca Frost
TOF
July 25, 2005 - January 21, 2009

Lukas Scott Smith
DILV
January 9, 2007

Luke Bajrami
HLHS
January, 15, 2008

Luke Robinson
Truncus Arteriosis/VSD
June 24, 2009

M

Madeline Mary Brodeur
Heterotaxy/Pulmonary Vein Stenosis
June 7, 2005 - August 31, 2005

Madison Ford Hutsell
TOF
October 17, 1991

Marcus Joetsootud "Joyful" Morton
Critical Aortic Stenosis (AS)/BAV
January 2, 2009

Matthew Stephen June
HLHS
April 15, 1997

A Special Honor to Alex's heart friends: CHD Survivor's & Angel's

Megan Stewart
HLHS
October 22, 2008

Meredith Annette Matt
3rd Degree Atrioventricular (AV) Block
January 19, 1990

Mia Grace Marrone
HLHS
April 29, 2010 - July 25, 2010
She had the Norwood May 5, 2010. She was doing great but earned her angel wings on 7/25/2010. They are unsure what went wrong. She was able to give us almost 3 whole months of memories. "Gone from our sight but always in our hearts!"

Micah Robert Muller
HLHS
March 13, 2007

Michael Joseph Pesco
HLHS/DORV/Heart Transplant Recipient
September 4, 1996

Michael Lawson
TOF/PS/possible Asperger's Syndrome
October 30, 2006

Michael Lee Jacobs
Shone's Complex
June 23, 2006

N

Nancy May Laverty
HLHS
September 3, 2008

Nevaeh Kaylene Walp
TOF/PA/MAPCA's/PFO(ASD)/Pulmonary Hypertension(PH)
September 17, 2006

Noah Ryan Durham
HLHS
February 12, 2010

O

Oliver Lane Ballmer
HLHS
August 14, 2008

Oliver Quezko Shelpman
HLHS/Heart Transplant Recipient/PS
April 6, 2007

Olivia Harvey
PS/COA/Mitral Valve Stenosis
December 19, 2002

P

Paula Kathryne Rieber
TOF/ASD
November 17, 2009

R

Rebecca Honican
TOF
August 23, 1982

Reece Skinner
Aortic Stenosis/BAV/small ASD
Novembe 3, 2010

A Special Honor to Alex's heart friends: CHD Survivor's & Angel's

Riley Brock
TGA
December 30, 2008

Rita Aguirre-Frankmore
Single Ventricle TA/TGA/PAH Cardiomegaly
July 1, 1966

Robbie Van Tine
VSD/ASD
May 18, 2005

Ronja T.C. Wodtke
HLHS
May 11, 1998

Ryder Carlin Allman
Sinus Venosus ASD, involving pulmonary vein
January 9, 2009

S

Sairah Grace Casto-Hodge
TGA/PS
October 19, 1992

Sammie Louis
HRHS/PA/Stroke Survivor
September 5, 2005

Samuel Hartley (Sammy Pants)
HRHS/PA
January 7, 2004

Sawyer Michael Brodeur
TGA
August 5, 2008

Scarlett Antoinette Pomaville
TOF/PA
February 17, 2009

Serena Lesley Cisneros
Hypertrophy Cardiomyopathy
August 25, 2009 - March 15, 2010

Seth Douglas Bonnett
HLHS
March 27, 2008 - October 12, 2008

Shawn Stockwell
HLHS/Heart Transplant Recipient
August 10, 1998

Shay Gammon
HLHS
January 15, 2001

Sophie Bernajeanne Woxland
HLHS
September 17, 2009

Sydnie Brown
TOF/PA/PH/DiGeorge Syndrome
November 23, 2001

T

Tadhg Addison Parenteau-Bouzane
TOF
May 15, 2009

Tanesha Mae Ives
Complete AVSD
May 31, 2009

A Special Honor to Alex's heart friends: CHD Survivor's & Angel's

Thomas Jensen
HLHS
January 29, 2001

Tiernan Flynn
Complete AV Canal/COA/Mildly Hypoplastic LV and Aorta
August 19, 2009

Tino Lorenzo De La Rosa
DILV
May 14, 2007

TJ Hunter Smith
TOF/DiGeorge Syndrome
August 2002

Travis Reyes
HLHS
November 24, 2009

Tristin Riley Fairbanks
HLHS
March 10, 2008 - May 20, 2008

Tristyn Michael Turner
Shone's Complex: COA/VSD/ASD/Sm. Mitral Valve/ BAV/Sm. Left Ventricle/bidirectional blood flow in his heart/Aortic/Sub-Aortic Mitral Stenosis
July 28, 2009

W

William Arrowsmith
PA/VSD/MAPCA's
November 22, 2004

Wyatt Hatcher
HLHS/Tricuspid Valve Regurgitation
October 20, 2008

X

Xavier Gallegos
HLHS
May 4, 2009

Y

Yasmin Southwood
TOF/VSD
May 21, 1985

Z

Zachary Mulvey Cardio
Myopathy Transplanted
January 4, 2001

Zachary Steven Botma
Truncus Arteriosus
February 23, 2007

Zachery Thomas Fields
PDA/ASD
July 19, 1993

Zachery Watkins
ASD/VSD/Pulmonary Vein Stenosis
February 4, 2004 - January 24, 2006

Zoe Elizabeth Chambers
Arotic Stenosis
December 12, 2005 – December 2008

Zoe Madison Lihn
HLHS
May 11, 2010

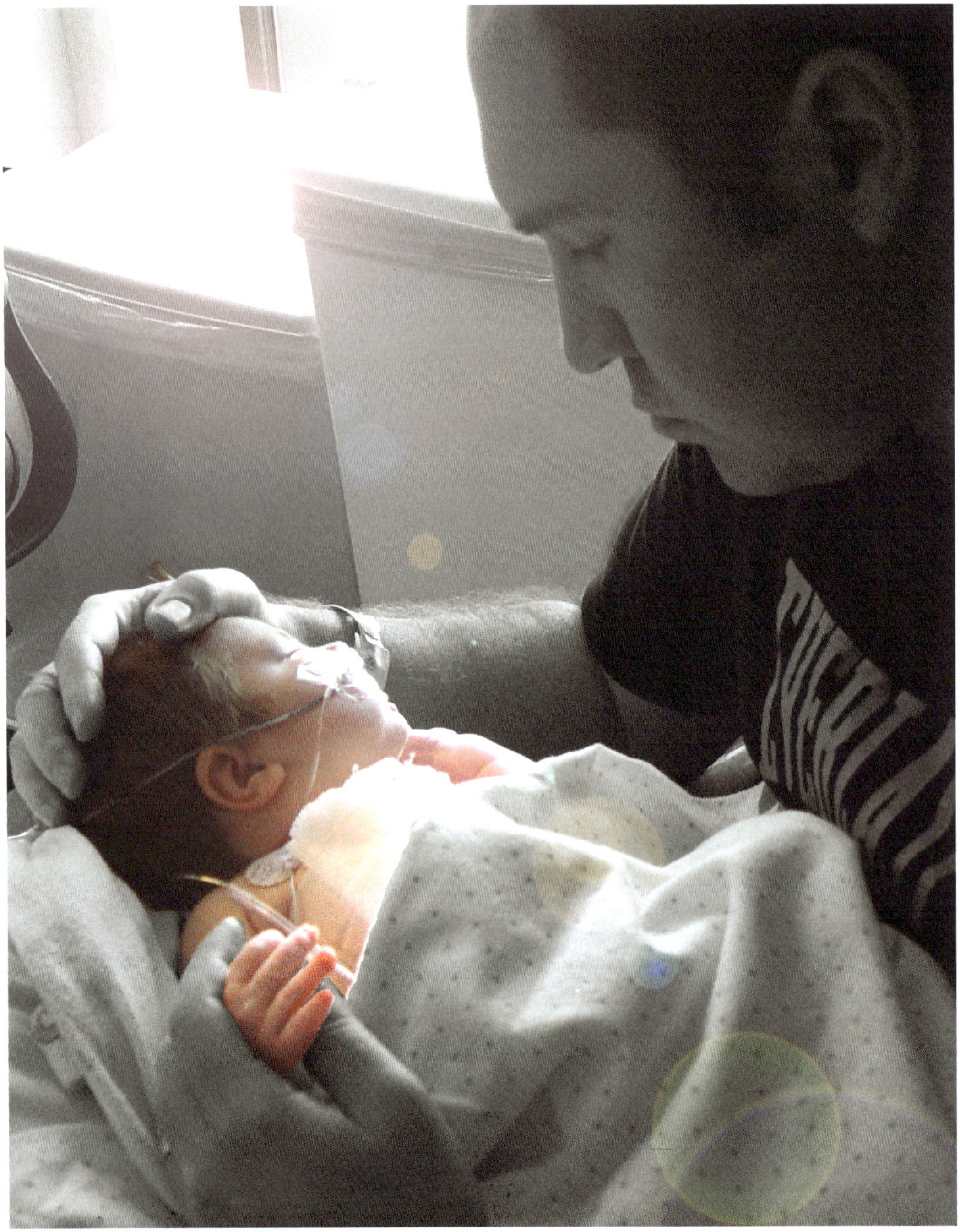

How to Make Donations

If you would like to make a donation to Alex's heart fund, please go to the Cedars-Sinai Medical Center Web page at http://www.cshs.org. Click on "Giving & Support" (at the top of the Web page). Then scroll down and click on "Gifts and Contributions" in the left margin. From here, you can click on "online" or "contribution form."

To make an online donation, click on "online," fill out the Donation Information section by filling in the dollar amount, and in the "designation" box, scroll to Heart Disease. Under Additional Information you have the option of checking the "Anonymous" box and entering your comments. Under Tribute Information, please write "Children's Heart Fund in Memory of Alexander Xavier Gallegos." You can also scroll to "In honor of" or "In memory of."

In the "Description" box, write "The Gallegos Family" if you choose to send a letter. This will allow us to send you a thank-you note for your generous contribution. This does not include the amount you donate, which is between you and Cedars-Sinai Medical Center.

To send a contribution by mail, please download, print, complete, and send the donation form with your gift. Please be sure to write "Children's Heart Fund in Memory of Alexander Xavier Gallegos" on the "Special Fund" line near the bottom.

Thank you for your support!

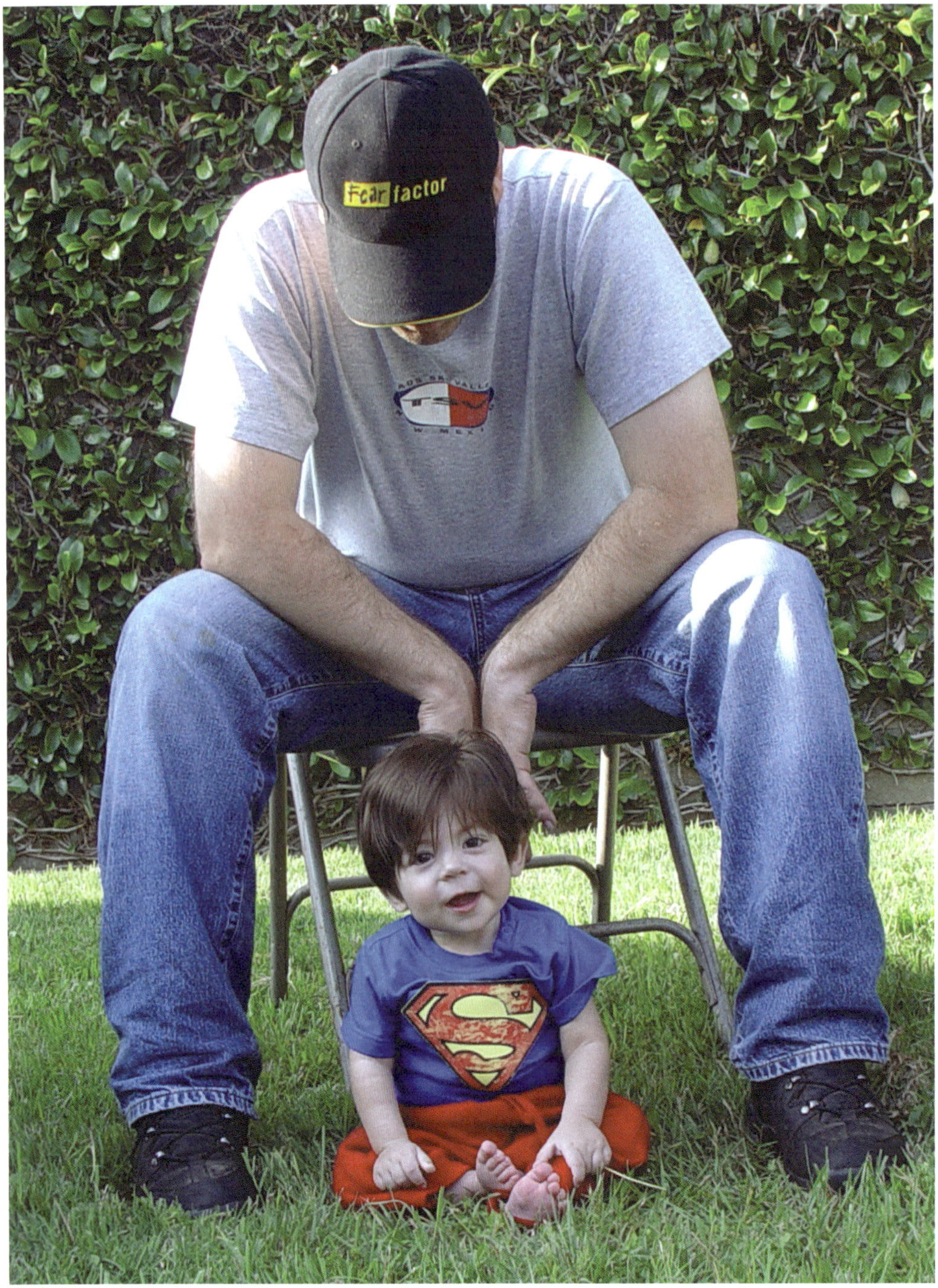
Fear factor

A Super-Special Thank-You Dedication

The Childrens' Heart Fund in Memory of Alexander Xavier Gallegos could not help the families of blue babies without the generous contribution and kindness from the "Lucas" family.

A heartfelt thank you for taking the time to get to know us and learn about Alex "The Old Soul" and "Wise One" and his heart condition.

We will be forever indebted to you and your family!

A Tribute to Alex's Doctors and Nurses

Thank you to Dr. Fontana, RN Anne, Dr. Fink, and your pediatric cardiac team for giving us time to get to know Alex. Thanks to Dr. Blank for his long-distance attempt to save Alex, our little angel. Without doctors like you, Alex would have not had the time to mesmerize us. There are no words to express our gratitude for your professionalism, skills and commitment to our son. We honor you and are grateful to you.

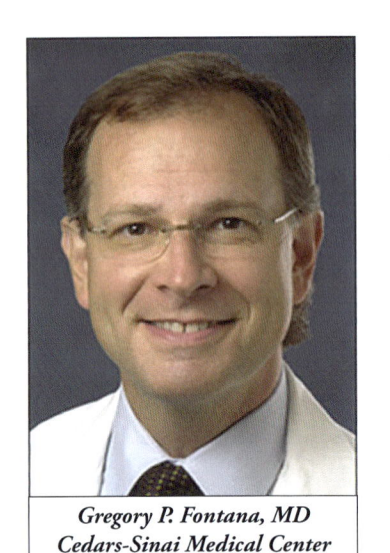

Gregory P. Fontana, MD
Cedars-Sinai Medical Center

Anne Hakes, RN, MSN, NP
Cedars-Sinai Medical Center

Burton W. Fink, MD

Harold N. Amer, MD
Cedars-Sinai Medical Center

David Blank, MD
Coastal Pediatric Medical Group, Inc.

Cameron Lowder,
BSN, CCRN

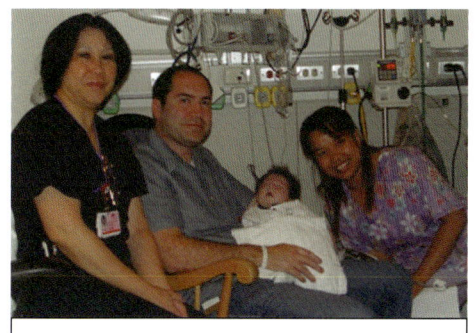

Gilda and Agnus my first nurses

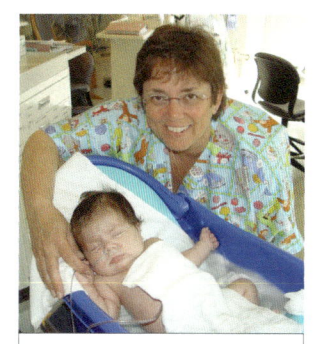

Judy Ostheimer, RN

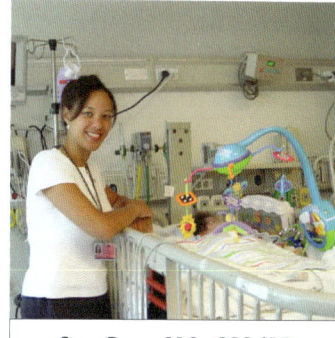

Stacy Payne, M.S., CCC-SLP

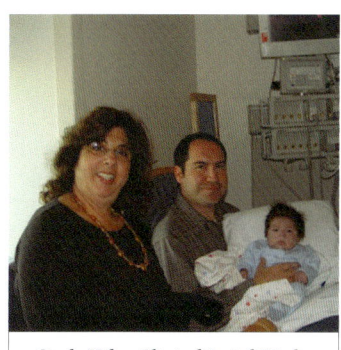

Cindy Hiles, Clinical Social Worker

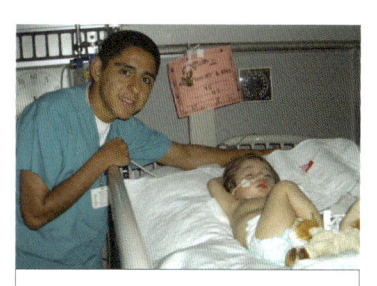

Transportation team Tony

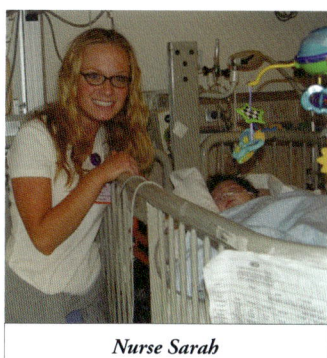

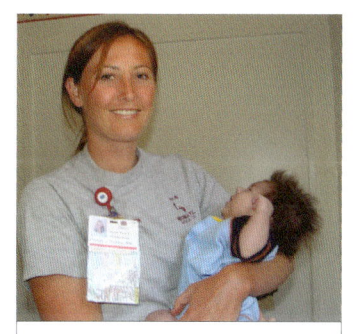

Nurse Sarah

Christy J. Dobbie, RN

Leaving with Alina NICU for PEDS

Andrea Raftery, PT

About the Author

Annette Gallegos was born and raised in Las Vegas, New Mexico. She received a Bachelor's Degree in Business Administration from the University of New Mexico, Anderson School of Management in May 1999. She is a stay-at-home mother and she is married to Rick Gallegos, a Civil Engineer. They currently reside in Ventura, California.

On June 7, 2005, Rick and Annette's son, Alex, was born with a congenital heart disease called Tetralogy of Fallot with Pulmonary Atresia. He was treated at Cedars-Sinai Medical Center. He remained in the hospital for two and a half months and was then released. Alex had to return to the hospital on his first birthday for additional treatment for his heart condition. After two years Alex suddenly became ill and passed away.

Ten months later on April 18, 2008, Alyssa was born. She was their little healer and helped them through the most difficult time of their lives. She was born a healthy and happy baby girl. Even though this book was written as if Alyssa were the older sister, she is actually Alex's younger sister.

Resources, support, advocacy and financial assistance for families and individuals affected by CHD:

www.alexheartfund.org
www.campdelcorazon.org
www.childrensheartfoundation.org
www.congenital-heart-defects.co.uk
www.hope4tinyhearts.com/hope
www.littlehearts.org
www.mattersoftheheart-online.com
www.tchin.org
www.tri-counties.org
www.kidswithheart.org
1-800-538-5390 toll free

Activity Page—Heart Puzzle

CPSIA information can be obtained at www.ICGtesting.com
Printed in the USA
BVIW12n1917171018
530473BV00010B/87